JOURNALLING THROUGH
EXODUS

WITH
THE DEVOTED COLLECTIVE

The Devoted Collective
Auckland, New Zealand
www.thedevotedcollective.org

© Copyright 2021 The Devoted Collective Ltd. All rights reserved.

ISBN: 978-0-473-67049-8

No portion of this book may be reproduced, stored in a retrieval system or transmitted in any form or by any means—electronic, mechanical, photocopy, recording or otherwise— except for brief quotations in printed reviews of promotion, without prior written permission from the author. All text in bold or in parentheses are the author's own.

Unless otherwise noted, all Scripture is taken from the New International Version®, NIV®. Copyright © 1973, 1978, 1984, 2011 by Biblica, Inc.™ Used by permission of Zondervan. All rights reserved worldwide.

Cover design by Holly Robertson of Design by Rocket www.designbyrocket.com
Book Illustrations by Marie Warner Preston of Outspoken Images www.outspokenimages.com
Compiled and edited by Aimée Walker

Cataloguing in Publishing Data Title: Reading Through Genesis
Author: The Devoted Collective
Subjects: Devotions, Christian life, Spirituality

A copy of this title is held at the National Library of New Zealand

*In your unfailing love you will lead
the people you have redeemed.
In your strength you will guide them
to your holy dwelling.*

Exodus 15:13

The Book of Exodus is often thought of solely as a story of rescue, but there is a far greater narrative for us to explore here: This is a book of invitation. An invitation to freedom, yes, but ultimately an invitation to meet with God and to behold His glory. Like Israel, we are being called out from the dominion of sin to become a people of His presence; a people who serve the Lord and His good purposes, worshipping Him alone.

In these pages, we will travel with the people of Israel, retracing their deliverance from Egypt and gleaning from their responses. We will see our own hopes, fears, and struggles reflected in theirs, and be reminded time and again of our own need for a Saviour and for the empowering work of Holy Spirit to live this new life that we are called to. And as we do, the question that we must answer is *How will we respond to God's invitation?* Will we be like the Israelites, keeping our distance and only seeking God for what He can do for us? Or will we be like Moses, drawing near to pursue intimacy with the Lord and going only where His presence leads so that our lives might also visibly reflect the glory of God?

It is our prayer that as you journal your way through Exodus with us, your understanding of Scripture will be expanded and enriched, the foundations of your faith strengthened, and your heart brought to a place of overflowing awe and gratitude for the goodness of our God. May you wholeheartedly say "yes" to this wonderous invitation and enter into the fullness of all that He has purposed for you.

The Devoted Team

Exodus in Context

To help you get the most out of your study of Exodus, we've compiled some background notes and tips for using this journal. Anchoring your observations in the correct historical and Scriptural context will enrich what you take away from your time in the Word and help you to build a solid theological foundation.

AUTHORSHIP

Exodus is the second of the five books that form the Torah (also known as the Pentateuch), all of which are attributed to Moses. However, unlike the first book Genesis, where Moses is neither mentioned nor an eyewitness of the events recorded, in Exodus Moses plays a leading role in the narrative and his authorship is clearly established within the text itself. For example, in Exodus 17:14 Moses is instructed to write down events so that the Israelites could remember them and in 24:4 we are told that he "wrote down everything the LORD had said." His authorship of Exodus is also supported by other books in both the Old and New Testaments.

DATING

Written in the last forty years of Moses' life, Exodus picks up where Genesis left off with the arrival of Joseph's family in Egypt, briefly summarising for us what has happened in the intervening years. It then focuses on a period of approximately eighty years from the birth of Moses through to the end of Israel's first year in the wilderness.

There are two possible time periods given for when the exodus itself took place: the 15th or 13th Century B.C. There are compelling reasons for both dates, but the 13th Century is often preferred for geographical reasons given that where the Egyptian pharaohs lived by this time would have made it possible for Moses to be going back and forth from the palace to confront Pharaoh. Furthermore, by then Egypt had lost possession of Canaan, which fits with the narrative that follows in Joshua, as the Israelites were not fighting Egypt for possession of the promised land.

AUDIENCE

It is likely that the original audience was the second generation of Israel who had grown up in the wilderness and were getting ready to enter the Promised land. But it is also intended to enable future generations—including us—to know and remember what the Lord had done on behalf of His people and to understand what it looks like to live in covenant-relationship with God.

GENRE

Exodus is classified as both historical narrative and law. In historical narratives, events from the past are retold for the benefit and guidance of another generation. They are true events whose primary purpose is to tell us what God did in the history of Israel—and this is particularly true of Exodus. The events that we will read define what it means to be an Israelite and should never be reduced to mythology, mere moral lessons, or simple allegories. As Terence E. Fretheim writes, "As a constitutive event, the exodus is recognised as an event of such import that the community would not be what it is without it having occurred."

When reading these accounts, it can be tempting to interpret them through our own cultural lens, judging them from our vantage point in history. But it is vital that we consider them in the context of the biblical authors, always remembering that they recorded events as they actually happened and not necessarily as they *should* have happened.

One of the things that can help us interpret this genre well is to keep God's universal plan in the forefront of our minds, asking the question: *How is the big picture story of redemption unfolding and how do the individual stories being told fit into it?* Because herein lies the crucial difference between biblical narratives and other narratives: This is God's story—and He, not us, is always the hero.

In addition to the Ten Commandments, Exodus also contains numerous laws that set out how they were to interact with God and one another. These sections of the book fall into the genre of law and must therefore be read through a different lens. Unlike the historical narrative, which is descriptive as opposed to prescriptive, the laws *are* concerned with what the people *should* do. They set out the conditions for being in covenant relationship with God and establish what it looks like to live as His people.

However, they too must be read in light of their historical and cultural context. For example, the very presence of a law permitting slavery (Exodus 21) might feel offensive to us now, but its stipulations were revolutionary in their time. They required them to act better than their neighbours who did not know God and reflected God's intention that all people ultimately be free. Where a law no longer applies to us, we can ask the question: *What is the deeper value of this law? What does it reveal to me about the nature of God?* And then allow the answer to shape our own behaviours.

STRUCTURE

There are various ways of viewing the structure of Exodus, each highlighting different themes and emphases for us.

For example, when focusing on characters, we might simply divide the structure into two: "The Saga of Moses" (chapters 1-4) and "The Saga of Israel" (chapters 5-40). Whereas if we focus on the primary theme of redemption we see the story developing in this way: the need for redemption (chapters 1-6); the might of the Redeemer (chapters 7-11); the character of redemption (chapters 12-18); the duty of the redeemed: obedience (chapters 19-24), and finally, provisions for the failings of the redeemed (chapters 25-40).

When approached on the basis of genre, the following structure helps us to make sense of how the book is organised:

Chapters 1-20: The continuation of the narrative begun in Genesis.
Chapters 21-24: The giving of the law.
Chapters 25-31: The detailed instructions for the construction of the Tabernacle.
Chapters 32-34: A return to the historical narrative highlighting how the Israelites' complaining progresses to full-blown idolatry.
Chapters 35-40: The instructions for the building of the Tabernacle are repeated before concluding with one last brief moment of narrative when the cloud of God's presence comes and covers the Tent of Meeting.

THEMES

Exodus details for us the deliverance of Israel from Egypt, but more than simply showing us what they were saved from, it teaches us what they were saved *for*: to dwell with God. At the heart of this book is the theme of redemption—what it requires and what it means to live as a redeemed people, set apart for the Lord.

As Exodus unpacks the theology of redemption it also explores numerous other important themes that deepen our understanding of Christ's work on our behalf, continually pointing us to the sovereign power of God and His divine purposes at work throughout all generations.

Firstborn

The theme of the firstborn can be traced from Genesis to Revelation, and in Exodus 4:22 we see an important development in this narrative when God claims Israel as His firstborn son. Exodus 12 and 13 further cement this theme when a lamb is offered first for the protection of the firstborn and then for their redemption when God calls for all the firstborn sons to be consecrated to Him. In all of this, we see Jesus foreshadowed, the firstborn of creation and of the dead (Colossians 1:15 and 18), and the Passover Lamb (1 Corinthians 5:7 and 1 Peter 1:19), who would one day offer Himself for our redemption that we, too, might be consecrated to the Lord.

Divine presence

Throughout the book of Exodus we see many contrasts with Genesis. In Genesis, we follow the history of a family, but here we trace the history of a nation. In Genesis, Abraham's descendants are few, but here they are numbered in the millions, and whereas once they were welcomed and honoured in Egypt, now they are feared and mistreated. But perhaps one of the most striking contrasts is that the manifest presence of God that was lost in Eden is restored to Israel, marking them out as a people belonging to God.

This theme begins in Exodus 3 with the burning bush and continues with the visible guidance of the pillar of cloud and fire and the theophany in Exodus 19 before culminating in the glory of the Lord filling the Tabernacle in Exodus 40, pointing us to the day when our bodies would become temples, and God would not only dwell with us, but *within* us.

Giving of the Law

Entwined with the theme of divine

presence is the giving of the law. The law establishes the Israelites' side of their covenant-relationship with God, teaching them how to live before a holy God.

SEEING JESUS IN EXODUS

From the moment Christ reveals Himself in the burning bush as the great "I AM," the presence of Jesus is tightly interwoven into the narrative of Exodus, and we are continually pointed to His work as our Redeemer through its rich typology and symbolism.

He is our Passover lamb and the unleavened bread; He is manna from Heaven, the rock that was struck for our salvation, and the ultimate temple through which God will forever dwell amongst His people. He alone is the means of our own deliverance from the unrelenting master that is sin into the freedom and wholeness of belonging to the Father and living as His beloved children. May Holy Spirit open the eyes of our hearts afresh to behold the wonder of all that Christ is and all that He has done on our behalf.

How To Use This Journal

This journal is organised into eight weeks of readings. Within each week, you'll find five days of readings and journalling pages, allowing two 'grace' days to catch up on any missed days and to reflect on what you've learned with our 'Week in Review' pages. The combination of lines and white space is designed to allow you to be creative in how you record your journey through Exodus. Illustrate a verse, ask the Spirit to draw with you, collage words that stand out—anything you feel moved to do!

Our journalling pages follow a pattern of *Observations*, *Obstacles*, and *Outcomes*. Start by reading the passage of Scripture in full. If you have time, consider going through it a few times to really get familiar with the nuances and details that are easily missed in a single pass. Once you have read the passage, you are ready to make your observations.

OBSERVATIONS

God's Word is a rich treasure trove, and no matter how familiar a passage may feel, there is always something more for us to discover there. As you slow down to make your observations, invite Holy Spirit to open the eyes of your heart and to give you insight and understanding. Then begin by noting the themes and connections you observe in the passage as a whole before working through verse by verse.

Questions you may find helpful to ask yourself:

When and where do these events take place?
Who is in this passage?
What is happening?
Why is it happening?
How are repetition, contrast, wordplay, symbols, etc. used to draw out meaning?
What themes are being developed?

What do these verses reveal about the character and nature of God?

Where is Jesus in this passage?

OBSTACLES

This section is your space to wrestle. As we read and study Scripture, it's important that we don't gloss over the hard parts. We need to be honest with ourselves about what we don't understand, what we struggle to reconcile with what we know about God, what feels contradictory with other parts of the Bible, and what might be difficult to implement. If we don't voice these things, doubt can begin to erode the foundations of our faith.

Each day, we encourage you to record the things you've read that pose an obstacle for you—whether it's an issue of understanding or outworking. Then, if you need to do some research to understand more fully, research. If you need to sit with the Lord and let Holy Spirit guide you, sit. Know that God is big enough to handle your questions and wants to empower you to walk in the truth of His Word. You might not always uncover the answers you're looking for immediately, but identifying the things you wrestle with starts the conversation and makes a space for Holy Spirit to instruct you in this area.

OUTCOMES

This is where we pause to consider the application of the passage in the context of our everyday lives. We don't want to simply consume information but to allow ourselves to be shaped and transformed by the words which ultimately point us to the Living Word: Christ. This will only happen if we recognise that God's Word is alive and active, understanding that while it has an intended application for its original audience, it also meets us where we are at today.

Take some time to reflect. *Is there something God is inviting you to do in response to what you have read? Something He is wanting to encourage you with at this time?* Write these things down and invite Holy Spirit to show you how you can practically outwork them.

Using 'the 3 Os' to study and meditate on the Word will help you draw closer to the heart of the Father as your understanding of His character, good purposes, and sovereign plans is enriched. May each day's reflection deepen your intimacy with the One who continues to call you to Himself.

WEEK ONE
EXODUS 1-5

Day One

EXODUS 1

OBSERVATIONS

OBSTACLES

OUTCOMES

Day Two

EXODUS 2

OBSERVATIONS

OBSTACLES

OUTCOMES

Day Three

EXODUS 3

OBSERVATIONS

OBSTACLES

OUTCOMES

# Day Four

EXODUS 4

OBSERVATIONS

OBSTACLES

OUTCOMES

Day Five

EXODUS 5

OBSERVATIONS

OBSTACLES

OUTCOMES

WHAT CHARACTERISTICS OF GOD WERE HIGHLIGHTED FOR YOU THIS WEEK?

HOW DID THE LORD ENCOURAGE AND CHALLENGE YOU THROUGH THIS WEEK'S READING?

WHICH OF YOUR 'OUTCOMES' IS GOD INVITING YOU TO PRIORITISE IN THE WEEK AHEAD? WHAT IS YOUR PART IN OUTWORKING IT?

WEEK TWO
EXODUS 6-10

Day Six

EXODUS 6

OBSERVATIONS

OBSTACLES

OUTCOMES

Day Seven

EXODUS 7

OBSERVATIONS

OBSTACLES

OUTCOMES

Day Eight

EXODUS 8

OBSERVATIONS

OBSTACLES

OUTCOMES

Day Nine

EXODUS 9

OBSERVATIONS

OBSTACLES

OUTCOMES

Day Ten

EXODUS 10

OBSERVATIONS

OBSTACLES

OUTCOMES

Week in Review

WHAT CHARACTERISTICS OF GOD WERE HIGHLIGHTED FOR YOU THIS WEEK?

HOW DID THE LORD ENCOURAGE AND CHALLENGE YOU THROUGH THIS WEEK'S READING?

WHICH OF YOUR 'OUTCOMES' IS GOD INVITING YOU TO PRIORITISE IN THE WEEK AHEAD? WHAT IS YOUR PART IN OUTWORKING IT?

WEEK THREE
EXODUS 11-15

Day Eleven

EXODUS 11

OBSERVATIONS

OBSTACLES

OUTCOMES

Day Twelve

EXODUS 12

OBSERVATIONS

OBSTACLES

OUTCOMES

Day Thirteen

EXODUS 13

OBSERVATIONS

OBSTACLES

OUTCOMES

Day Fourteen

EXODUS 14

OBSERVATIONS

OBSTACLES

OUTCOMES

Day Fifteen

EXODUS 15

OBSERVATIONS

OBSTACLES

OUTCOMES

WHAT CHARACTERISTICS OF GOD WERE HIGHLIGHTED FOR YOU THIS WEEK?

HOW DID THE LORD ENCOURAGE AND CHALLENGE YOU THROUGH THIS WEEK'S READING?

WHICH OF YOUR 'OUTCOMES' IS GOD INVITING YOU TO PRIORITISE IN THE WEEK AHEAD? WHAT IS YOUR PART IN OUTWORKING IT?

WEEK FOUR
EXODUS 16-20

Day Sixteen

EXODUS 16

OBSERVATIONS

OBSTACLES

OUTCOMES

Day Seventeen

EXODUS 17

OBSERVATIONS

OBSTACLES

OUTCOMES

Day Eighteen

EXODUS 18

OBSERVATIONS

OBSTACLES

OUTCOMES

Day Nineteen

EXODUS 19

OBSERVATIONS

OBSTACLES

OUTCOMES

Day Twenty

EXODUS 20

OBSERVATIONS

OBSTACLES

OUTCOMES

WHAT CHARACTERISTICS OF GOD WERE HIGHLIGHTED FOR YOU THIS WEEK?

HOW DID THE LORD ENCOURAGE AND CHALLENGE YOU THROUGH THIS WEEK'S READING?

WHICH OF YOUR 'OUTCOMES' IS GOD INVITING YOU TO PRIORITISE IN THE WEEK AHEAD? WHAT IS YOUR PART IN OUTWORKING IT?

WEEK FIVE
EXODUS 21-25

Day Twenty-One

EXODUS 21

OBSERVATIONS

OBSTACLES

OUTCOMES

Day Twenty-Two

EXODUS 22

OBSERVATIONS

OBSTACLES

OUTCOMES

Day Twenty-Three

EXODUS 23

OBSERVATIONS

OBSTACLES

OUTCOMES

Day Twenty-Four

EXODUS 24

OBSERVATIONS

OBSTACLES

OUTCOMES

Day Twenty-Five

EXODUS 25

OBSERVATIONS

OBSTACLES

OUTCOMES

WHAT CHARACTERISTICS OF GOD WERE HIGHLIGHTED FOR YOU THIS WEEK?

HOW DID THE LORD ENCOURAGE AND CHALLENGE YOU THROUGH THIS WEEK'S READING?

WHICH OF YOUR 'OUTCOMES' IS GOD INVITING YOU TO PRIORITISE IN THE WEEK AHEAD? WHAT IS YOUR PART IN OUTWORKING IT?

WEEK SIX
EXODUS 26-30

Day Twenty-Six

EXODUS 26

OBSERVATIONS

OBSTACLES

OUTCOMES

Day Twenty-Seven

EXODUS 27

OBSERVATIONS

OBSTACLES

OUTCOMES

Day Twenty-Eight

EXODUS 28

OBSERVATIONS

OBSTACLES

OUTCOMES

Day Twenty-Nine

EXODUS 29

OBSERVATIONS

OBSTACLES

OUTCOMES

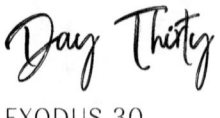

EXODUS 30

OBSERVATIONS

OBSTACLES

OUTCOMES

Week in Review

WHAT CHARACTERISTICS OF GOD WERE HIGHLIGHTED FOR YOU THIS WEEK?

HOW DID THE LORD ENCOURAGE AND CHALLENGE YOU THROUGH THIS WEEK'S READING?

WHICH OF YOUR 'OUTCOMES' IS GOD INVITING YOU TO PRIORITISE IN THE WEEK AHEAD? WHAT IS YOUR PART IN OUTWORKING IT?

WEEK SEVEN
EXODUS 31-35

Day Thirty-One

EXODUS 31

OBSERVATIONS

OBSTACLES

OUTCOMES

Day Thirty-Two

EXODUS 32

OBSERVATIONS

OBSTACLES

OUTCOMES

Day Thirty-Three

EXODUS 33

OBSERVATIONS

OBSTACLES

OUTCOMES

Day Thirty-Four

EXODUS 34

OBSERVATIONS

OBSTACLES

OUTCOMES

Day Thirty-Five

EXODUS 35

OBSERVATIONS

OBSTACLES

OUTCOMES

Week in Review

WHAT CHARACTERISTICS OF GOD WERE HIGHLIGHTED FOR YOU THIS WEEK?

HOW DID THE LORD ENCOURAGE AND CHALLENGE YOU THROUGH THIS WEEK'S READING?

WHICH OF YOUR 'OUTCOMES' IS GOD INVITING YOU TO PRIORITISE IN THE WEEK AHEAD? WHAT IS YOUR PART IN OUTWORKING IT?

WEEK EIGHT
EXODUS 36-40

Day Thirty-Six

EXODUS 33

OBSERVATIONS

OBSTACLES

OUTCOMES

Day Thirty-Seven

EXODUS 37

OBSERVATIONS

OBSTACLES

OUTCOMES

Day Thirty-Eight

EXODUS 38

OBSERVATIONS

OBSTACLES

OUTCOMES

Day Thirty-Nine

EXODUS 39

OBSERVATIONS

OBSTACLES

OUTCOMES

Day Forty

EXODUS 40

OBSERVATIONS

OBSTACLES

OUTCOMES

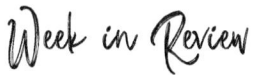

Week in Review

WHAT CHARACTERISTICS OF GOD WERE HIGHLIGHTED FOR YOU THIS WEEK?

HOW DID THE LORD ENCOURAGE AND CHALLENGE YOU THROUGH THIS WEEK'S READING?

WHICH OF YOUR 'OUTCOMES' IS GOD INVITING YOU TO PRIORITISE IN THE WEEK AHEAD? WHAT IS YOUR PART IN OUTWORKING IT?

About the Devoted Collective

Our vision is simple: to wholeheartedly pursue the 'more' of God together.

This looks like serving God with wholehearted devotion, fulfilling the command Christ gave us to love the Lord with all our heart, soul, and mind (Matthew 22:37).

We want to love God with all that we are right where we are. In order to do that, The Devoted Collective is anchored in three core disciplines modelled for us in Acts 2:42: devotion to the Word, to community, and to prayer. It is our heart's desire that, through committing to these practices with us, you will experience the richness of all God intends for your life as you come to know Him more intimately.

The more we know God, the more we can't help but love Him; and the more we love Him, the more we'll desire to partner with Him to establish it on earth as it is in Heaven. And that's what wholehearted devotion is all about. It's about living into the MORE of God.

Connect with us:

Website: www.thedevotedcollective.org
Socials: @thedevotedcollective

Join Us in the Devoted Community

We want to invite you to be part of The Devoted Community.

A curated online space hosted by Elim accredited Pastor Aimée Walker and Go + Tell Gals Certified Coach and Pastor, Em Tyler, The Devoted Community is an intentional discipleship hub away from the busyness and stress of social media, that will equip, empower, and release you into all that God has for you and help you build a resilient relationship with your God. It's where you'll find a company of women to cheer you on and a toolkit of resources to help you grow and go deeper with God.

WITHIN OUR COMMUNITY YOU WILL FIND:

Bible reading plans
Interviews & Teaching videos
Prayer threads and small groups
Dedicated mentors and monthly lives with Aimée and Emily
Exclusive content
Access to our digital courses
Downloadable study guides & journals
Believers seeking the heart of God—just like you

WHO IS IT FOR?

If you are hungry and thirsty for more of Jesus...
If you desire to go deeper in your faith...
If you want to take hold of all the promises of God...
If you yearn for your faith to make a difference every day...
If you long to enjoy Him all the days of your life...
If you are looking for others who feel the same...

...then The Devoted Community is for you.

Let's pursue the MORE of God together:

www.thedevotedcollective.org/community

www.ingramcontent.com/pod-product-compliance
Lightning Source LLC
Chambersburg PA
CBHW072336300426
44109CB00042B/1638